THE BUOYANCY OF SPACE

Poems by Gill Nicholson

For Ibby,
long time dear friend
& fellow poet;
with love,
Gill.
xx.

HEN·RUN

First published in 2014 by Hen Run
An imprint of Grey Hen Press
PO Box 450
Keighley
West Yorkshire
BD22 9WS
www.greyhenpress.com

ISBN 978-0-9926983-0-0

Printed by Flexpress, Birstall, Leicester LE4 3BY

For David

Acknowledgements are due to the magazines and journals in which some of these poems have been previously published:

Obsessed with Pipework; Poetry News; ARTEMISpoetry; Other Poetry

I am deeply indebted to *Small Handful* – Jennifer Copley, Ann Wilson, Rachel Rycroft, Jo Stoney and Kim Moore, to Mark Carson and *4th Monday Poets*, to *Barrow Writers* and to Kendal's *Brewery Poets*, for their constructive suggestions and encouragement. Also to Phil Johnson Laird, Caroline Gilfillan and Caroline Carver who have supported me long distance. Their help has been constant and invaluable. First and foremost I owe this collection to my late husband David Bell Nicholson, who saw me through numerous re-drafts with poetic intelligence and devotion.

Contents

Waking to a hat-box

I woke up to the hatbox –
broad-brimmed straw
with yellow feathers and a satin trim.
Sunbeams lit the ceiling
and the floor was warm beneath my feet.

Outside a breeze was spinning leaves
into the wheel spokes
of my rusty bike. I put
my house-coat on and went
into the scullery to feed the cat.

I phoned my sister
and we laughed together at the thought
of what the day might bring.
The marigolds I'd picked the day before
had opened in the breakfast room.

Post shuffled through the letterbox –
my daughter's tumbled handwriting
and reassurance she would bring her frock,
and I was notified that finally,
the date was set.

The Big One

- speak of shabby childhoods –
W.H. Auden.

A celebration's taking place,
a drunk exchange that looks like rivalry
and an exaggerated grovelling –
her family is on its knees
mopping up the sloshed champagne.

By lunch, rat-arsed,
they're finding fault and throwing stones
that cause a bruise the size
of whispers in a language
of their own.

They leave with arms thrown in the air,
hiss at her, you're not one of us.
Her night's a wreck.

When next they meet
you'd think she'd seen a shrink
she's so all there.

They look at her with open eyes,
heads on one side:
Are you all right?
Her answer's what they want to hear:
I'm fine, she says.

Night Train

Those nights she's lost
inside a labyrinth
of winding corridors,
floors reached by stairs
which have no banisters.
It's end of term.

She finds an open door,
goes down stone steps to city streets
lit up. She must get home.
She searches for the station,
map, ticket office, cash.

Someone says a train is due
but there's no destination she recalls.
Her brain's a beetle on its back.
She has a thick pink ticket saying
LONDON and RETURN.

She's on the train.
Her ticket's clipped. She opens up
a grease-proof packet on her lap.
The train stops. She's ordered off.
It's after midnight. Moonlight picks
like torchlight at her brown attaché case.

It splits, spills pens,
her stamp album, her swaps.
They flutter down the platform
on the wind like ragged moths.

The train spews steam. She leaves
in gritty clouds that hide the moon.
Shadows flit like movie shots
across a pavement and an empty road
that curves away.

Our Dead Are Still Dead

but they strain towards us,
comb knots from our hair,
make us yell, eyes watering.

They lay their heavy hands
upon our backs, and, though
we clamp our teeth, replay
scenes we've been burying.

They're dead, but still we hear them
splutter as we shoulder
the percussion of remarks:
that's typical of you -

why can't you just -
as if by doing what we're told
they'll love us more.

They are as still as earthquakes,
these still dead, who rise up
through our shattered roads.

Submerged Cathedral
after Debussy

In bays, in summertime, small lilies bloom,
tall rushes wave their silver heads
and warblers call.

Below, detritus floats ghosted by plumes
from pulsing gills, and in the chilly gloom
the pike lies almost still.

Through sodden doors dream-people drift,
rise to the clerestory. One touches fan-vaults
stroked by undertow and wonders at their form.

Some sway in prayer, read death-dates carved
on tombs of rusty ancestors.
Small children find in colour-dazzle of glass

traced figures in the parables they've known.
Old soldiers grasp a tattered regimental flag,
recite the names of comrades lost in consecrated wars.

Sceptics show their scars and sneer, point fingers
at disjointed history. At dusk a thin moon
rises to the surface of the lake.

The Art of War

Dispatched to our recycle bins
the women, children and their plastic bags
to be composted images and bulletins.

A naked napalm victim's peeling skin,
arse-kicking goose-steps and salutes to flags
dispatched to our recycle bins

with flattened cities, shrapnelled bodies sinking
into mud, the queues of refugees in rags
to be composted images and bulletins.

A hundred severed heads an oligarchy's whim,
the last remains of sons beneath white slabs
with flower trim, dispatched to our recycle bins

and Armageddon in a backpack, hiding
legs, an eye, death to your daughter or your dad
to be composted images and bulletins.

There's buzz enough – devising battles we can't win.
Our super weaponry's recycled tragic acts
are caught before dispatching to the bins
to be composted images and bulletins.

Hostages

We see the livid elderly
strike in madness,
strong as in their youth,

smell the dread of fearful ones
who sweat at death, not for themselves
but for the ones they try to sooth
with morphine day and night.

We watch the silent dispossessed
in foreign camps who have to beg,
walk through mud, contaminated
canisters of water in their fists.

We know an alcoholic,
see him pissed and pissed on –
observe him as he falls and falls, until
nobody wants to know.

Who wouldn't step around these vagrants,
refugees, the deranged old,
who wear their hopelessness like armour,

sigh words for thirst and hunger
we can't understand. They whisper them,
their sullen voices edged with emptiness.
They are as helpless as the stars.

Of Steps on Snow
after Debussy

We stand beside the cold white glaze
that covers everything
except this stone – our starting point –
don't want to break the surface
or leave tracks that show
we've been here, seen the hazards,
felt the bite that warms our bones,
the flush that follows on.

This love's enough to make you shake –
you want to pick it up, press it
to your heart, but know how it could fall
apart, drop through your fingers;
how its settled flakes will melt, a trail
of footprints mark its brittle skin.

Giardini

After the film by Steve McQueen, Venice Biennale 2009

Too old for racing now, five brindled greyhounds
poke through rubbish scattered on the grass
or trapped in cracks. At six a.m. she lets them out
to find the winter's rain has sluiced the roofs,
set off new scents.

The turtle-woman pulls her trolley full of cat-food
round corners as routinely as the dogs remember sex.
A beetle inside tree roots clambers out for air,
its crimson carapace caught by this nosing camera.
The park is destitute; each nation's show-place
shuttered up.

Yet in some pebbles, bright as a clutch of marbles,
yellow cinquefoil grows. A worm stretched through
the water of a pool is shot in close up:
its ridged elastic body moves as though
the centuries have stopped.

At dusk, lamps light up walkways
bare of art's contemporary shows.
Drops ping cold glass; drip down, drip down,
as fruitless trails make puddles whose reflections
turn back only on themselves.

Two church bells chime, collide and then divide.
At midnight, shadows breathe. A cigarette glows.
Maybe a man is waiting. Out of the dark,
he lifts his arms and holds another in the silence,
a question that the camera shares.

Dawn comes again. Lights go out, reveal black trees
that regiment the avenues. He catches it: the moment
when the spider hides against a muted bark.
Sun will come out, birds flick their wings and twitter,
dogs, their muzzles down, will search.

Veils
after Debussy

Cobwebs loop, span tarn-side reeds.
You break their thread without regard
and though you know they must be there
you can't believe the mesh exists until
the mist drifts down at dawn. You see them
when the morning rag drips everything with dew.
The tarn itself is veiled, its surface calm,
dark as a shade and leaden in its depths.

A wind blows the meniscus, rakes it
into waves that catch the rising sun.
The shade is ripped to tattered rills,
scraps transformed to sparkling stars.
Not done, quick breezes grab the chance
to jettison their silver breath.

Gathering Water-Lilies

from a photograph by Dr P Emerson

In sepia, deep shadows blank their faces.
He, in a country hat, has braces hauling up
his rough twill trousers to his chest.

She wears a broad-brimmed straw
her bodice tight, embroidered skirt
voluminous around her knees,

leans in the stream, plucks water-lilies out
to bundle in her other hand.
What business they're about seems leisurely.

With oar-grips held in toughened hands
he lets the lighter glide, the current's drift
to shift them with stealth

through channels filled with plates of green
and reeds that bend in unison, their sturdy boat
just able to negotiate the narrow waterways.

Before day's end they'll pile the flowers in a net,
will dangle it, oars resting quietly,
until the tench swim in, lured by the blooms.

Hard to imagine how, when now they are so still,
the man will flick his wrist and haul the fish
its weight as great as ugliness of form

and when it's caught on board
she'll give a shriek and clutch the hull,
then thump its head, be jubilant there's one to kill.

Wild Fruit

after photographs by Deborah Parkin

She wants to capture us,
instructs us to be still,
hang our heads and close our eyes.
We think she'd eat us if she could.

We try to hide behind the trees –
this is our secret corner of the wood;
we even wear our masks
but she can see through them.

When we're asleep she traps us,
strokes our cheeks
and wraps us in her arms.
She tries to keep us close.

This happens each September
when the crab apples and elderberries
tell her that the time has come
for us to go away again.

An Autumn Sunday in the Grass Market

The old man's there again.
He's cleaning up religiously –
his sacramental tools a tiny brush
and trowel worn fine with use.
Down on his knees he scrapes
the cobble-cracks and brushes up
the cigarette butts, ring-pulls,
grit and last night's chips, folds
them tight in paper tossed from takeaways.

He carries every parcel to the waste bin,
stuffs them in beyond his elbows.
When his altar's neat and clean,
each fallen leaf retrieved,
he signs in lines drawn
in the soil below the trees:
two on each side of each square bed.
His service has no end,
his dogged bending, genuflexion
to the season's wantonness.

Ifs and Ands

If weather changes radically
and it gets hotter than we've known,
will butterflies and moths grow
big as peacocks?
Will a businessman who swelters
in a steaming office, dream
he's standing in tall grass,
a net big as a parachute
held in his hand
his small fat legs whipped
to a frenzy as he swish-swashes,
traps the monster tiger moths,
the meadow browns like eagles,
purple emperors like herons,
but all lightly flitting on the wing;
and will he laugh and laugh
collapsing in the meadows
stripping off his togs,
not caring who is watching
as he lies there face up
to a cloudless day?

As December Is Too Dark

we recreate the autumn now –
red, gold with green, a bower
of leaves. We hoard rare fruits,
wrest kernels from their shells,
light candles, dusky incense – all
mementos of the season gone.
We even recreate the sparks
that rime the naked trees,
twist skeins of cable plugged
to flash and flow with fables
we all know, and kid ourselves
with cheerfulness, our cheeks
turned pink as though somehow
the cold has warmed to alcohol,
and so, punch-drunk and spiced,
we churn the old refrains
until December lumbers off
and with a minute turn
days dawn as silver January.

Now, the Dark Rain

I bend under the umbrella
into the stone porch
and through the heavy wooden door.

It's been so many years.
I slide into a pew, nod
either side and look

towards the altar steps
no coffin… a memorial.
The girls file in,

a fat man I don't recognise.
He is the son, the little boy –
we're by a mill-stream, picnicking

and they are paddling.
Rain beats on this roof,
but now the rain

is dark rain,
your long red hair
turned ashen

and you're bowed
your face deep-shadowed,
yet your mouth

as I have seen before,
firm as a line drawn
under tearfulness.

Your hands contain the hymnbook
and I see you singing
but no sound

and afterwards, waiting
as we pour towards you –
I'd forgotten how statuesque.

Grief adds to that.
You shoulder it as if the weight
is keeping you afloat.

Last Letters

i.m. John B.

Last time we met he shook
and wiped saliva from his lips.
Now there's cancer in the prostate gland.

He lives alone, writes about his partner –
how her secret life lies hidden
in the pages of her favourite books.

Bach helps to float his days,
the garden too, which flourishes,
although its vigour worries him.

The photo that he takes and makes into a card –
snow-laden tree of heaven in the winter sun –
is processed expertly, although

his signature's a spring that's come unfurled.
He says his partner's shadow stays with him
and now is his.

Unsaid

It lives inside my secretaire,
in files I save,
in cards I've kept to read again;
it lives between my curtains
and these faded walls,
antiques and pictures that I bought;
it lives in every day I go downstairs
gripping the banister.

It lives in forms petitioning
the way I want to go;
in surgeons covering their backs,
my name against the surgery;
it lives inside the pills I take,
the tea to swallow them;
it lives inside forgotten words
and faces that I ought to know,
my awkward smile the giveaway.

Apart

Coming at you right from the start,
love on its breath
all rich and creamy,
till you taste its undertones.

Coming with words like *wait*,
all will be well
and *not what you thought*,
not creamy now, but aloes.

Your stomach's tense with fear.
You have been warned
to keep away because it's dark.
Some rooms are out of bounds.

But you're alert – a voyager –
creep in to find a sea up to your chin.
You learn to swim,
tread, breathe more slowly.

And you find your twisting way,
but oh, you are alone, because
your lovers and your children each
has to do what you have done.

Time brings the lonely meetings,
hungry meals, but then they wave
because they have to go.
It's over and it's not enough.

Sea Shanties

We sing for those in peril on the sea
as breezes skid across the paddling pool.
I'm in my woolly bathing suit. I choose
a patient-looking donkey, trust the man,
his dog, suppose my parents' love. Now time's
a telescope. They wave, say how you've grown!

School trip to Whitby Nab. I've grown
into my sister's clothes. Now-a-days you see
how storms tore down the Nab, how time
and waves remember shale and pools
where winkles that we gathered, cling. The man
I marry buys a yacht. He'll choose

the East coast route – choose
not to hire the pilot at the river's mouth. I groan,
am sick and hanging on. This madman
sails wind-over-tide. I lurch above the sea
and swirl. At anchor, not much safer in the pool
of cabin light, I fear I'll drown. Now time's

a river and I have a baby son. Sometimes
I fear for him. Maybe one day he'll choose
the Hilo route, but here, loose cattle stand in pools.
Tides lick the beach. My son grows
tall, sets strings of hooks deep in a silver sea,
hauls tigered mackerel skilfully as any man.

Mid-voyage Sirens croon to tempt a man
who's landed on the Isle of Skye in wintertime.
We meet, this man and I, in winds that cut, seas
scattered in a glancing sun. We choose
to throw our contracts into clouds – have grown
light-headed in the dazzle of these frozen pools.

Years on we take the sea wall, cross the pools
below the viaduct, pass gullies where a fisherman
competes with sharp-billed birds. I've grown
infirm, reach for that steady hand. Our time's
the wrong end of the telescope. We choose
to idle, watch the Leven churn into the sea.

See us laughing at our ancient faces in a pool.
Time empties on the breaking wave. How old I've grown.

The Vigil
i.m. Sybil Bensusan

They brought along her oxygen supply
though all that afternoon she sat
without it, watched, her eyes as heedful
to our moves as if she was an avid fan
and we the players of her chosen game.
She hardly spoke. She seemed too angry,
too determined to hang on to what was said,
the chat, the jokes, shared memories,
to waste her breath on explanations,
reassuring words she knew were not the point.
It was as if we were the dying ones
and she the mourner keening over us.

Dud

and if they catch me weeping
I can say I'm weeping over Dud –
today I saw him play
Beethoven Bogey on Utube,
revealing every classical cliché
with wicked eyes
and flashing grin.
He kept on glancing up at me
knowing I would marvel
at his technical bravura,
thumping out the coda
till you thought he'd burst
or that the keys would fly apart,
the dampers split their sides,
the body of his Grand collapse,
and how he said to Terry,
I can't speak but I can play,
sliding mock exhausted to the floor.
I laughed and laughed,
and then I wept to think of him
in later life reduced
to speechlessness.
So if they catch me weeping
I can say I weep for Dud
and yes, it's true, I do,
but really, who I'm weeping for
is you.

Dudley Moore CBE 19th April 1935 – 27th March 2002.

His Garden

After the scattering
she locks the doors on visitors
and every morning
in her dressing gown
wanders round the flower beds.

The roses have gone over,
yet are showing buds again.
Soon the autumn rains will come,
rot them on their foolish stalks.

Wet days she seeks the summerhouse,
rocks the chair he chopped the rockers off.
She sees his cuttings in their trays,
how at last they've rooted deep,
strong enough to plant outside.

She'll never soil her hands
or bend her back for them.
Perennials grow thick
and crowd the beds,
fall over on the weedy paths.

She crushes them beneath her feet,
sniffs advancing ground elder,
laughs at bindweed coiling stems
of phlox and canterbury bells.

All These Heavy Books
with acknowledgements to W.H. Auden

pressed in their shelves
like rigid butterflies on pins.

You hear the fustiness
which crusts each page
like dust that once exploded
in a city blitz, their patina
no more than déjà vu.

And yet you cleave to them
like leaves on winter twigs,
believe they hold the sum
of all you've been.

Are they god-like volumes
preaching with double tongues?
Tomb-stones you would have
around as touch-stones?

Or do they whisper through
the rustle of page after page
Get rid of us, for where you go
words hold no weight? By then
you'll know the buoyancy of space.

No Longer

I no longer trust the sun
however mistily it rises
or how brilliantly it slips down in the west.

I no longer trust the tides,
winds, water drops or crystals falling
however they're described.

I don't trust clouds
no matter how they're shaped or patterned
and I've never learnt to trust the sea.

Add the mountains, fells,
the water meadows, buttercups,
rivers running loose and noisily

with caddis larvae hauling houses
on their backs, however they are built –
sand, wood or stone.

I've lost trust in the pike,
know, like the rest, the minnows
will betray me.

What's more, I've lost trust in the sky
because I know it's going to fall –
a black and clammy winding sheet,

and though I'll struggle under it
it's going to wrap me and my loved ones up,
dissolve us like the rest.

Gill Nicholson has lived in South Cumbria for fifty years. She taught in mainstream and special education, and had her own pottery studio. This collection stems from her retirement and the twenty years lived in her present home working alongside her second husband, David. Her work references her past, questions the future and the predicaments of aging, always with an eye on nature and landscape. Latterly she has experimented with set forms and poems inspired by music, photography and art. Her poems have been anthologised, and widely published in magazines including Pitch, Pennine Platform, The Interpreter's House, Seam, Iota, Other Poetry, Artemis & Poetry News. Gill's first collection is Naming Dusk in Dead Languages (Handstand Press 2010).